THE FEDERALIZATION OF PRESIDENTIAL PRIMARIES

THE
FEDERALIZATION
OF
PRESIDENTIAL
PRIMARIES

AUSTIN RANNEY

American Enterprise Institute for Public Policy Research
Washington, D.C.

Austin Ranney is a resident scholar of the American Enterprise Institute and a member of the Democratic National Committee's Commission on the Role and Future of Presidential Primaries.

Library of Congress Cataloging in Publication Data

Ranney, Austin.
   The federalization of Presidential primaries.

   (Studies in political and social processes)
(AEI studies ; 195)
   1.   Presidents—United States—Nomination.
2.   Primaries—United States.   3.   Political
parties—United States.   I.   Title.   II.   Series.
III.   Series: American Enterprise Institute for
Public Policy Research.   AEI studies ; 195.
JK522.R36   329'.022'0973   78-56292
ISBN 0-8447-3297-4

AEI Studies 195

Printed in the United States of America

CONTENTS

1
Renewed Interest in Federalized Primaries

Legislative proposals to federalize the legal machinery for nominating presidential candidates are neither new nor urgent. The first was a bill introduced in 1911 by Representative Richmond P. Hobson (Democrat, Alabama) proposing that presidential candidates be nominated by direct national primaries regulated by law rather than by national conventions regulated by party rules. Since then, well over 250 bills have been introduced in Congress, including thirteen in 1977, the first year of the 95th Congress. Yet, in all these years, floor action has been taken on only three of the proposals (in 1947, 1950, and 1952), none has ever come close to passing either chamber, and none of the 1977 bills even got out of committee.[1]

Why, then, bother discussing them? There are, I believe, excellent reasons for doing so now. One is that in the late 1970s proposals for some kind of federalized presidential primaries are being discussed more widely and seriously than for decades. Another is that the volume of such discussion is likely to increase rather than diminish.

Impact of the New Delegate-Selection Rules

The new concern is, I believe, an unanticipated consequence of the sweeping changes made in the governing rules and strategic nature

I am grateful to Leon D. Epstein, Jeane Kirkpatrick, and Howard R. Penniman, all of whom made useful comments on early drafts of this paper.

[1] The numbers, sponsors, and introduction dates of all bills for federalizing presidential primaries introduced from 1911 to 1976 are listed and their contents categorized in Joseph B. Gorman's useful *Federal Presidential Primary Proposals* (Congressional Research Service, Library of Congress, JK 2071 A 76-53 G, 1976). For the bills introduced in 1977, I have made use of the compilation by the staff of the Democratic National Committee's Commission on Presidential Nomination and Party Structure.

of the presidential nominating process since 1968. The first round of changes, promulgated by the Democratic party's McGovern-Fraser commission in 1969, were intended to transfer control of the process among Democrats from the party's "bosses" and their "organization followers" to people actively supporting a particular candidate or policy in a particular presidential year. Most of the commissioners were convinced that this goal would be accomplished far better by a reformed convention than by a national primary. The right kind of convention, they declared, would be better than a national primary in two respects:

> In view of the stringent demands made upon a President of the United States, the challenge imposed upon any contender for the nomination in seeking support in a wide variety of delegate selection systems should be maintained.
> The face-to-face confrontation of Democrats of every persuasion in a periodic mass meeting is productive of healthy debate, important policy decisions (usually in the form of platform planks), reconciliation of differences, and realistic preparation for the fall campaign.[2]

Accordingly, the commission's guidelines sought to ensure that all convention delegates, whether selected by state caucuses and conventions or by state primaries, would be chosen in a manner that would give "all Democratic voters . . . a full, meaningful and timely opportunity to participate."[3]

In 1968, seventeen states (including the District of Columbia as a "state") chose or bound their national convention delegates by direct primaries. Altogether these delegates cast 37.5 percent of the convention's votes. The other thirty-four states and five territories chose their delegates by state conventions and committees, and they accounted for 62.5 percent of the votes.

After 1968, however, the proportions changed considerably. In 1972, the number of states using presidential primaries rose to twenty-three, and the proportion of convention votes determined by primaries rose to 60.5 percent. And in 1976, the numbers rose again to thirty and 72.6 percent, respectively.[4] Most of the fourteen states which

---

[2] Commission on Party Structure and Delegate Selection, *Mandate for Reform* (Washington, D.C.: Democratic National Committee, 1970), p. 12.

[3] Ibid., p. 9. For more detailed summaries and analyses of these reforms, see Austin Ranney, *Curing the Mischiefs of Faction: Party Reform in America* (Berkeley: University of California Press, 1975); and William J. Crotty, *Political Reform and the American Experiment* (New York: Thomas Y. Crowell Company, 1977).

[4] See Austin Ranney, *Participation in American Presidential Nominations, 1976* (Washington, D.C.: American Enterprise Institute, 1977), Table 1, p. 6.

adopted presidential primaries after 1968 did so as a direct response to the McGovern-Fraser rules. Some decided that primaries were the best way to provide genuine "full, meaningful and timely participation." Others decided that the best way to keep the new national delegate-selection rules from upsetting their accustomed and preferred ways of doing state and local party business would be to establish a presidential primary and thereby split off presidential nominating matters from all other party affairs. And still others calculated that the new rules made caucuses and conventions much more vulnerable than a primary to being captured by small but dedicated bands of ideologues.

Whatever the reasons for the proliferation of state primaries, the result was a process that some commentators by the mid-1970s regarded as the worst of all possible worlds. The "bosses" and "regulars" lost control in both 1972 and 1976. The ideological activists won it in 1972 but lost it in 1976. Consequently, some who still favored control by bosses or activists began to consider seriously whether a national primary, with all its disadvantages, would not be better than the 1976 system. For example, in the earlier editions of their distinguished analysis of presidential politics, Nelson Polsby and Aaron Wildavsky had praised the 1968 mix of conventions and primaries as about right. But their 1976 volume was not so sure:

> The great disadvantage of national primaries is that they weaken the main intermediaries between the people and their government—political parties. But if the existing and evolving presidential nominating process also weakens parties, and if it, in addition, enthrones purists over politicians, then given this unfortunate choice, a more direct relationship between candidates and their countrymen might be the lesser evil.[5]

Relation to Proposals for Abolishing the Electoral College

A closely related and reinforcing development is the renewed drive for a constitutional amendment abolishing the Electoral College and substituting direct election of the President without regard to state lines. The principal proposal in 1977 was S. J. Res. 1, sponsored by Senator Birch Bayh (Democrat, Indiana) with over twenty cosponsors. The concept of Bayh's proposal, if not all of its details, received strong support from such powerful organizations as the Chamber of Commerce, the AFL-CIO, and the American Bar Association, and

---

[5] Nelson W. Polsby and Aaron Wildavsky, *Presidential Elections*, 4th ed. (New York: Charles Scribner's Sons, 1976), p. 226.

3

such prominent individuals as Senators Hubert Humphrey, Edward Kennedy, Howard Baker, Robert Dole—and President Carter himself. Moreover, public opinion polls have consistently shown that well over two-thirds of the general population favor direct national election of the President.

A point often overlooked is that most of the arguments against the Electoral College and in favor of direct national elections can also be made against the national party conventions and in favor of a direct national primary. For example, the Electoral College is said to violate the one man/one vote rule of apportionment because it reflects the equal representation of the states in the Senate. So do the national conventions, for each state delegation's voting strength is based in part on the state's electoral votes. For another, the arithmetic of the Electoral College is said to create a serious danger that the candidate with fewer popular votes will be elected over the one with more popular votes. The same is true of the national conventions, which may nominate candidates preferred by only a minority of their parties' rank and file. Most important of all, the Electoral College is said to be an artificial device thrust between the sovereign people and their choosing of a President. It can serve only to distort the expression of their will, while direct election will always reflect that will clearly and accurately. By the same token, the national conventions are artificial devices inserted between rank-and-file party members and the choice of their presidential nominees. The conventions too can only distort the members' will, while a direct national primary will always reflect it faithfully. Finally, the idea of a direct national primary has as much public support as proposals for direct national elections: a Gallup Poll released in February 1976 showed 68 percent favoring a national primary in contrast to only 21 percent preferring the national conventions.

For all of these reasons, then, the idea of federalizing presidential primaries is of more concern to more people in the late 1970s than ever before, and it seems likely to attract more, not less, attention in the years immediately ahead. But there is a second and better reason for examining these proposals now. Even if they draw no nearer to enactment in the next few years than they have in the past, the proposals raise a number of tough issues about what our political system is and should be. Moreover, the proposals cut through these issues in unusual ways that help us understand them better.

Accordingly, this study has three objectives: to describe the principal types of proposals for federalized presidential primaries; to outline the main issues they raise; and to estimate the likely costs and benefits of each proposal.

4

2
The Proposals

Presented in order of increasing degrees of federal control are the following main proposals for federalizing presidential primaries introduced in 1977.

Restricting Dates for State Primaries

The least federal control provided by the various proposals is that envisioned in H.R. 4329, introduced by Representatives Morris K. Udall (Democrat, Arizona) and John Ashbrook (Republican, Ohio), both former presidential contenders.

Under this proposal each state decides for itself whether to hold a presidential primary, but if a state chooses to hold a primary, it must conform to certain federally imposed standards. First and most important, the primary must be held on one of only four prescribed dates—the second Tuesday in March, April, May, or June of the presidential year. Second, while a state may choose either a closed or an open primary, it must hold a presidential preference poll. Third, the Federal Election Commission must compile a national list of candidates, including all who are entitled to receive federal matching campaign funds, and all candidates on the list must be on the ballots in all states (additional candidates may win places by petition on any state ballot). Finally, all candidates who win 10 percent or more of the preference poll votes must be allocated delegates in proportion to their shares of the votes.

Regional Clustering of Optional State Primaries

A somewhat greater degree of federalization is proposed in S. 1207, introduced by Senators Bob Packwood (Republican, Oregon), Mark

Hatfield (Republican, Oregon), and Ted Stevens (Republican, Alaska). S. 1207 closely resembles bills introduced by Senator Packwood in 1972, 1973, and 1975; H.R. 3410, introduced by Representative Lee Hamilton (Democrat, Indiana); and H.R. 757 introduced by Representative Charles E. Bennett (Democrat, Florida).

As in the Udall-Ashbrook bill, each state is left free to decide for itself whether or not to hold a presidential primary. However, if a state decides to hold a primary, it has no choice of date; rather, it must use the date the Packwood-Hatfield-Stevens bill stipulates for *all* the states in its region.

The states and territories are allocated among five regions (the Hamilton bill provides for six). The first regional primary is held on the second Tuesday of March, and seventy days prior to that date the Federal Election Commission determines by lot in which region the first primary will be held. The other regional primaries are held on the second Tuesdays of April, May, June, and July, and the date for each region is determined by lot by the FEC seventy days before each date.

All states are required to restrict voting in each party's primary to that party's registered members, and states that do not have party registration are required to establish it.

The Federal Election Commission compiles a list of all the generally recognized presidential candidates, and these candidates must appear on the preferential poll ballot of every state (any aspirant not on the list may get on the ballot in each region by petition).

Every candidate who receives 5 percent or more of the votes cast in each state's preference poll must receive a share of the delegates proportional to his share of the popular votes. The delegates are required to vote at the convention for the presidential candidate to whom they are pledged for two ballots or until the candidate's share of the convention votes falls below 20 percent or until the candidate releases them. The vice-presidential candidates are selected by whatever procedures the conventions choose. And each state is reimbursed by federal funds for the costs of holding its presidential primary.

Compulsory State Primaries in Regional Groupings

A substantially greater degree of federal control is proposed by H.R. 4519, introduced by Representative Richard Ottinger (Democrat, New York). The Ottinger bill closely resembles the Packwood-Hatfield-Stevens bill, with one major difference: it *requires* every state to hold a presidential primary, while S. 1207, like H.R. 4329, leaves that decision up to each state.

The Ottinger proposal assigns each state to one or another of five regions (the allocation is identical with that proposed in S. 1207). Primaries are held in all the states in successive regions on the first Tuesday of April and on the Tuesdays of the third, sixth, ninth, and twelfth succeeding weeks, ending in June. As in S. 1207, the FEC determines by lot the order in which the regions vote. The FEC holds each "drawing" twenty days prior to the next scheduled date.

The ballot in each state must include all persons whom the FEC has declared eligible for federal campaign matching funds. Other aspirants may also get on the ballots in particular states by submitting petitions to the secretaries of state or equivalent officers.

The bill requires that in all states each party's primary must be closed to all but registered members of that party and directs the FEC to prescribe a system of party registration for any state that does not already have it.

The bill's provisions for proportional allocation of delegates, binding the delegates' votes at the convention, selection of vice-presidential candidates, and reimbursement of the states for the costs of holding primaries are all identical to those in S. 1207.

In short, the Ottinger proposal is identical with the Packwood-Hatfield-Stevens proposal with the one major exception, that the former requires all states to hold presidential primaries under conditions laid down by federal law, while the latter imposes these conditions only on states which have chosen for themselves to hold primaries.

Direct National Primary

The greatest degree of federalization is contained in the proposals to remove presidential nominations entirely from party conventions by holding a one-day direct primary over the entire nation without regard to state lines. This is not only the oldest reform proposal (the Hobson bill of 1911, noted above, proposed a national direct primary) but also the most frequent: about half of all the 250-plus bills on the subject call for some version of a direct national primary.[6] The versions introduced in 1977 include: H.R. 2063, introduced by Representative Joseph Gaydos (Democrat, Pennsylvania); S. 16, introduced by Senator Lowell Weicker (Republican, Connecticut); H.R. 6819 and H.R. 8717, both introduced by Representative Robert Leggett (Democrat, California); H.R. 1628, introduced by Representative Charles Carney (Democrat, Ohio); and H.R. 6865, introduced by Representative Albert Quie (Republican, Minnesota).

---

[6] Gorman, *Federal Presidential Primary Proposals.*

I shall focus mainly on the Quie proposal. This bill provides that "the official candidates of political parties for President and Vice President shall be nominated at a primary election by direct popular vote." Moreover, "the time of such primary election shall be the same throughout the United States," and the bill sets the date as the first Tuesday after the first Monday in August of presidential election years.

Like most of the other bills, H.R. 6865 calls for a closed primary, though it makes no provision for federally supervised party registration. Senator Weicker's bill, however, allows persons registered as independents to vote in the primary of either party.

The candidates acquire positions on the ballot by filing with the president of the Senate petitions bearing a number of signatures equal to at least 1 percent of the total number of popular votes cast in the nation for all candidates in the most recent presidential election. Candidates for vice-president must petition separately and appear on the ballot in a separate group. Moreover, no person may run for both the presidential and vice-presidential nominations.

Any candidate receiving a majority of the popular votes in a party's presidential primary becomes its official nominee. If no candidate receives a majority, a runoff election is held four weeks later between the two candidates receiving the most votes, and the one who wins a majority in the runoff is the nominee. The same conditions hold for the vice-presidential primaries. (The Gaydos bill allows a candidate to win the first primary with 45 percent or more of the votes, but the others require absolute majorities.)

These four types of proposals, then, are the main alternatives now suggested to replace the present system of nominations by national party conventions composed of delegates chosen by a variety of state-controlled primaries and caucus-convention systems. We now turn to an examination of the main arguments for and against the status quo and the proposed alternatives.

3

The Legalities

The various proposals for federalizing presidential primaries all pose the same constitutional questions: (1) does Congress have the power to regulate the manner in which presidential elections are held, or do such regulations require a constitutional amendment; and (2) does whatever power Congress has to regulate presidential general elections include the power to regulate presidential primaries? We shall consider both in the context of the hardest case—the uniform direct national primary ignoring state lines, as in the Quie proposal.

The Constitution's Words

We might begin by noting that all the bills introduced in 1977 propose acts of Congress, not constitutional amendments. So their sponsors evidently believe Congress already has full power to federalize the presidential nominating system as much as it wishes.

But *does* it? A nonlawyer's casual glance at the Constitution suggests that it does not. The two most relevant passages are:

> Article II, Section 1: Each state shall appoint, in such a manner as the legislature thereof may direct, a number of electors. . . . Article II, Section 2: The Congress may determine the time of choosing the electors, and the day on which they shall give their votes. . . .

These words say nothing at all about primary elections or any other device for presidential *nominations*, and for general elections they appear to give Congress only the power to specify the day on which electors are to be chosen and the day on which the electors are to cast their votes. But lawyers and judges see nuances in the words of constitutions which escape the myopic layman; and it is the lawyers' interpretations we must heed.

Interpretations

The second question posed above is easily disposed of: in *U.S.* v. *Classic*, the Supreme Court held that Congress's power to "make or alter" the laws regulating "the times, places and manner of holding elections for senators and representatives" (Article I, Section 4.1) applies to primary elections just as much as to general elections.[7] This judgment has been little disputed since, so it is clear that Congress has full power to regulate both primary and general elections for members of Congress.

But what about primary elections for President? The words in Article II quoted above leave considerable doubt about whether Congress has the same power over presidential elections. However, a series of pronouncements by the Supreme Court has resolved enough of these doubts for it to seem likely that the Court would uphold the constitutionality of the Quie bill or any other legislation establishing a national direct presidential primary. The Court's principal statements follow.

In *Burroughs* v. *United States* in 1934, the Court upheld an act of Congress that required the reporting of contributions to and expenditures by political committees in presidential elections. Justice Sutherland, writing for the Court, said:

> The President is vested with the executive power of the nation. The importance of his election and the vital character of its relationship to and effect upon the welfare and safety of the whole people cannot be too strongly stated. To say that Congress is without power to pass appropriate legislation to safeguard such an election from the improper use of money to influence the result is to deny to the nation in a vital particular the power of self protection. Congress, undoubtedly, possesses that power, as it possesses every other power essential to preserve the departments and institutions of the general government from impairment or destruction, whether threatened by force or by corruption.[8]

In 1970, Congress intervened even more drastically in the regulation of presidential elections by requiring that the minimum voting

---

[7] U.S. v. Classic, 313 U.S. 299 (1941), especially at 314-317.

[8] Burroughs v. United States, 290 U.S. 534 (1934), at 545.

age in elections for all federal offices, including the presidency, be lowered to eighteen. The Court's opinion of the act's constitutionality was not entirely clear, and in any event, it was superseded by the adoption of the Twenty-Fifth Amendment in 1971. But Justice Black, in giving the Court's opinion on the constitutionality of the 1970 law, declared:

> I would hold, as have a long line of decisions in this Court, that Congress has ultimate supervisory power over congressional elections. Similarly, it is the prerogative of Congress to oversee the conduct of presidential and vice-presidential elections and to set the qualifications for voters for electors for those offices. It cannot be seriously contended that Congress has less power over the conduct of presidential elections than it has over congressional elections.[9]

Finally, the Federal Election Campaign Act, enacted in 1971 and amended in 1974 and 1976, imposes many regulations on gathering and spending funds in presidential primaries. Even more, Congress provided for federal funding, on a matching basis, of presidential primary campaigns. This was surely based on Congress's very broad interpretation of its powers to regulate presidential primaries. The act's constitutionality was challenged on many different grounds. Significantly, however, no one argued that Congress has no power to regulate presidential primaries. The Court's *per curiam* opinion remarked on this fact:

> The constitutional power of Congress to regulate federal elections is well established and is not questioned by any of the parties in this case. Thus, the critical constitutional questions presented here go not to the basic power of Congress to legislate in this area, but to whether the specific legislation that Congress has enacted interferes with First Amendment freedoms or invidiously discriminates against nonincumbent candidates and minor parties in contravention of the Fifth Amendment.[10]

---

[9] Oregon v. Mitchell, 400 U.S. 112 (1970) at 124. A contrary view is possible. Justice Harlan's dissent argued: ". . . the fact that it was deemed necessary to provide separately for congressional power to regulate the time of choosing presidential electors and the President himself demonstrates that the power over 'Times, Places and Manner' given by Art. I, s. 4, does not refer to presidential elections but only to the elections for Congressmen. Any shadow of a justification for congressional power with respect to congressional elections therefore disappears utterly in presidential elections." (Ibid., at 211-212).

[10] Buckley v. Valeo, 424 U.S. 1 (1976), at 13-14.

In sum, then, it seems clear that Congress has full constitutional power to establish any of the four types of federalized presidential primaries reviewed above.[11] The question now becomes, *should* it? And if so, which type? Many issues should be considered before these questions are answered. Some of the most important follow.

---

[11] The same conclusion is reached by two legal scholars: James F. Blumstein, "Party Reform, the Winner-Take-All Primary, and the California Delegate Challenge: The Gold Rush Revisited," *Vanderbilt Law Review*, vol. 25 (1972), p. 975; and James Shinn Graham, "One Person–One Vote: The Presidential Primaries and Other National Convention Delegate Selection Processes," *Hastings Law Journal*, vol. 24 (1973), p. 257.

4
The Issues

Participation

Ever since the triumph of the Progressive movement in the early twentieth century, one of the criteria by which Americans have most often judged their political institutions is that of participation: does (or will) the institution facilitate and stimulate the widest possible participation by ordinary people in its affairs?

Why do so many set such store by participation? Several reasons are most often given: Popular participation is the best way to keep government honest, responsive, and responsible. Participation not only keeps government in line but makes it *seem* to be in line, which increases the people's confidence in its fairness, honesty, and legitimacy. Since human beings are civic animals, political participation is important for the full development of their uniquely human potential.

These are all factual propositions which may or may not be confirmed by the evidence. No matter; they are widely and strongly held articles of faith which set much of the tone in evaluations of our political institutions. By the participation criterion, the proposals for compulsory state primaries and for a direct national primary are clearly preferable to the present system and to the proposals for restricted dates or regional clustering of optional state primaries. They would require that a primary election be held in *every* state and the District of Columbia, while the optional proposals would probably mean that some states would eschew primaries in favor of caucus and convention systems. Universal primaries would certainly mean a major increase in participation. In 1976, for example, presidential primaries were held in twenty-nine states and in the District of Columbia. These thirty jurisdictions included an estimated 103,149,000 of the nation's total voting population of 136,538,000—or 75.5 percent of the total. Assume, moreover, that the other states had also held primaries in 1976 under either the Ottinger or the Quie plan and that their composite voting turnout had been the same as that in the states that did hold primaries (28.2 percent). The additional primaries would have raised the total number of participants from the 28,925,000 who actually did vote to a projected 38,504,000.[12]

That would have been a major increase, and those who measure participation, as most commentators do, simply by the *number* of people who participate in whatever fashion are likely to hail it as a major reason for enacting the Ottinger or Quie proposals. However, some advocates of "participatory democracy" do not agree. They say we should be concerned less with the volume of participation and more with its *quality*. And they generally prefer the kind of participation seen in caucuses and conventions to the kind which takes place in primary elections. A good example is this statement by political scientist Wilson Carey McWilliams:

> It seems to me that a convention system, firmly based on the grass roots, offers more genuine democracy and participation of higher quality than any direct primary can ever do. With proper guarantees of easy access at the precinct or sub-precinct level, an ascending series of local meetings culminating in a state convention (Iowa is something of a model here) offers a number of small, face-to-face meetings in which genuine deliberation is possible. . . . Such a system tends to decrease the power of the mass media and to emphasize commitment, organization and personal contact.[13]

This argument was often heard in the meetings of the Democratic party's latest reform commission (the Winograd commission) in 1977.[14] Its two predecessor commissions had rewritten the rules for selecting delegates to the national conventions so as to maximize the access and influence of people enthusiastic enough about a cause or a candidate to work actively well beyond the minimal involvement of voting in a primary. One of the main—and unanticipated—consequences of the new rules was the sudden increase in the number of states holding presidential primaries. Many members of the Winograd commission were not at all happy with this result and sought

---

[12] The data on which these statements are based are presented in Ranney, *Participation*, Tables 2 and 3, pp. 16, 20.

[13] Wilson Carey McWilliams, "Down with Primaries," *Commonweal*, July 1, 1976, p. 429.

[14] The group was officially named the Commission on Presidential Nomination and Party Structure but was usually called the Winograd commission after its chairman, Morley Winograd.

ways of diluting or reversing it. One said, "There is, to be sure, a question of participation here; but there is a question of leadership too." And another proposed that some way be found to limit the number of states permitted to hold presidential primaries.[15]

The argument underlying their position runs something like this: Voting, while necessary for registering preferences and making decisions, is by itself an undemanding, even superficial, form of participation. It requires only minimal motivation, effort, commitment, and knowledge. The voting act is performed alone, in private, with no confrontation of opposing views or discussion of any kind. Thus it is not only the most passive form of participation but also the least responsible. Attending a party precinct caucus, on the other hand, takes more effort, requires more motivation, and takes up more time. Persons attending must pay attention to several issues and deal with opposing points of view. They may even have to speak up for their preferred positions and against opposing ones. So participation in caucuses and conventions is of much higher quality than voting in primaries. It is therefore likely to produce greater personal development, a stronger sense of efficacy, and better grounded and more durable support for the political system. In short, any benefit claimed for participation in primaries is much more likely to result from participation in caucuses and conventions.

The argument seems persuasive enough, but it also cuts in some ways its advocates may not welcome. After all, it took a lot of energy, motivation, and effort for the old-fashioned party "bosses" and their "henchmen" to conduct their business in the "smoke-filled rooms" of prereform tradition. The activity of the typical participant was probably even greater, and it certainly was more frequent, than that of the middle-class reformers of the Progressive era and the issue/candidate enthusiasts favored by the Democrats' reform commissions. To be sure, the bosses supported different kinds of candidates and causes than those dear to the reformers. But if intense participation by the highly motivated few is to be preferred to passive participation by the weakly motivated many, why should it not be activity by bosses and henchmen rather than middle-class ideologues?

However that may be, this much, at least, is clear: A number of studies have shown that political activists of the sort who attend precinct caucuses and state conventions or become delegates to national conventions are quite different from ordinary party identifiers. The activists have substantially more education and higher incomes;

---

[15] I served as a member of the commission, and the quotations in the text are taken from my notes of its deliberations.

they are much more politicized—that is, they know more about political issues and feel more intensely about the policies and candidates they prefer. Often they are ideologically more extreme than their less active fellow partisans. In general, they are quite unrepresentative of their party's rank-and-file identifiers.[16]

What about the people who vote in presidential primaries? Any answer to that question must begin with the fact that turnout in primaries is almost always low—indeed, it is generally no more than half the number who vote in the ensuing general elections for the same office. For example, the presidential primaries between 1948 and 1968 produced an average turnout of 27 percent compared with an average turnout of 62 percent in the ensuing general elections. In 1976, the average primary turnout was 28 percent, while the turnout in November was 53 percent.[17]

In short, the primary electorate is ten times as large as the caucus-convention electorate—but only half as large as the electorate in general elections. How representative is it? The few studies of this question suggest that each party's primary voters are unrepresentative of its rank-and-file identifiers in the same ways as the caucus-convention activists but not to the same degree.[18]

It is clear, then, that the "selectorate" in a federalized presidential primary system—especially one that required primaries to be held in all the states—would not only be much larger than any up to now but also would include higher proportions of less interested, less ideological, and less knowledgeable people. Accordingly, even more than at present, the selectors would depend upon the mass news media to learn who the "serious" candidates were, to identify the political stance and personal character of each, and to keep score on who was winning and losing. And this, in turn, would profoundly influence many other aspects of the presidential selection process.

The Nature of Campaigns

Some advocates of federalized primaries argue that the "crazy quilt" character of the present scattering of the primaries' states and dates

---

[16] Two recent studies making these points in detail about national convention delegates are: Jeane J. Kirkpatrick, The New Presidential Elite (New York: Russell Sage Foundation and Twentieth Century Fund, 1976); and Denis G. Sullivan, Jeffrey L. Pressman, Benjamin I. Page, and John J. Lyons, The Politics of Representation: The Democratic Convention of 1972 (New York: St. Martin's Press, 1974).

[17] Ranney, Participation, p. 24.

[18] See Austin Ranney, "Turnout and Representation in Presidential Primary Elections," American Political Science Review, vol. 66 (1972), pp. 21-37.

requires the candidates to crisscross the nation repeatedly, which increases travel costs and wears down the candidates' health.[19] There is something in this, but most commentators are more concerned about the quality of campaigns than about the inconveniences of campaigning.

From the candidates' standpoint, of course, the main function of a primary campaign is to win votes. From the voters' standpoint, a primary has several functions. One is to provide the voters with the information from which they may readily learn as much as they wish about the personal character and issue positions of each candidate. This function is especially important in campaigns for primary elections because, unlike general elections, primaries do not place party labels beside the candidates' names to help the voters distinguish the good guys from the bad.

Some analysts believe that the present mix of primaries, caucuses, and conventions performs the informing function poorly. For example, Malcolm Jewell argues:

> We know very little about what factors influence the choice of voters in presidential primaries, but there is evidence that the voters are often poorly informed about the views on issues and those candidates whose names have only recently become household words. For example, polls have shown that Eugene McCarthy won more votes from hawks than from doves [regarding the Vietnam war] in the 1968 New Hampshire primary. There is evidence that voters' perceptions of McGovern were not clearly formed early in the 1972 campaign, and that many of them began to perceive him as a "radical" only after most of the primary elections were over. It is not true that most voters do not care about the issue orientation of candidates. (The Wallace candidacy is a case in point.) It is true that voters are likely to develop perceptions about issue positions rather slowly, only after they have become familiar with the candidate's image and style. The structure of the presidential primary system makes it possible for a candidate to win primaries if he has a strong organization, plenty of funds, shrewd advisers, an appealing campaign style, and a good image on television, even if his position on issues is not well known and is likely to antagonize many voters once they become familiar with it.[20]

---

[19] See, for example, Representative Lee Hamilton, *Congressional Record*, February 9, 1977, pp. H1026-7; and Senator Lowell Weicker, *Congressional Record*, January 10, 1977, p. S177.

[20] Malcolm E. Jewell, "A Caveat on the Expanding Use of Presidential Primaries," *Policy Studies Journal*, Summer 1974, p. 282.

Others have noted that the formless, personalistic character of primary contests impels candidates to seek ways other than policy stands to differentiate themselves from their opponents. Judson James correctly points out that

> the candidates must make themselves known to an apathetic electorate and differentiate themselves from their opponents. Therefore, a dramatic slogan and/or personality are tempting approaches, as also is an emphasis on divisions within the party. A frequent tactic in primary campaigns is to exploit the popular antagonism against party organization. People can be distracted from other issues by a successful attack on the opponent as the candidate of the "bosses."[21]

Polsby and Wildavsky add that, in a multicandidate national primary,

> since all contenders would be wearing the same party label, it is hard to see how voters could differentiate among candidates except by already knowing one or two of their names in favorable or unfavorable contexts, by liking or not liking their looks, by identifying or not identifying with their ethnic or racial characteristics, or by some other means of differentiation having nothing whatever to do with ability or inclination to do the job, or even with their policy positions.[22]

Some proponents of federalized primaries contend that they will improve the quality of campaigns by eliminating the kind of local demagoguery encouraged by the present hodgepodge of locally determined dates. With a few nationally fixed dates or a single date, it is said, all candidates would be forced to address national issues all the time.[23] Yet it seems to me that (1) the national news media will cover only the "leading national candidates" in any future system as they do at present, and the decision about who merits such coverage will remain theirs alone; and (2) what they report will continue to constitute what the campaign *is* for most voters everywhere. If that is the case, the events and statements the media choose to report and what they say about who is gaining or falling back are likely to be more important, now *and* in the future, than the legal structure of the primary system.

Some opponents argue that federalized primaries will keep the

---

[21] Judson L. James, *American Political Parties: Potential and Performance* (New York: Pegasus, 1969), pp. 70-71.

[22] Polsby and Wildavsky, *Presidential Elections*, p. 221.

[23] See Representative Lee Hamilton, *Congressional Record*, February 9, 1977, pp. H1026-7.

candidates close to television studios in New York or Los Angeles, and the grass roots will neither see nor hear any discussion of issues of local concern.[24] Yet this does not happen in campaigns for presidential *general* elections, which have one federally fixed date, so there is no reason to believe it would happen in a federalized presidential primary system.

In short, whatever gains federalized primaries might produce in lowered travel costs and reduced wear and tear on the candidates, they seem likely to have little impact on the nature of prenomination campaigns or their utility as devices for helping the voters make informed choices.

Candidates Favored

It is no secret that in presidential nominating politics as in any other contest, rules are not neutral. Any set of rules is bound to favor candidates with certain assets over those with other assets. Consequently, any change in the rules is bound to help some candidates and hinder others. But how?

Most analysts agree that the present *sequenced series* of state primaries maximizes the chances that a little-known or "outsider" candidate will become a major contender by first doing well (that is, better than expected—by the news media) in the early primaries and caucuses and then building visibility and attracting workers and campaign contributions on that base. This was the story of Eugene McCarthy in 1968, George McGovern in 1972, and Jimmy Carter in 1976.

By the same token, a one-day national direct primary probably could be won only by a contender already well known and well financed. As William Keech and Donald Matthews put it:

A primary can have a multiplier effect far beyond the borders of the state in which it takes place. The massive national publicity that the presidential primaries receive makes it possible for a little-known politician to become a national figure by a strong showing in a single state and go on to capture convention delegates in other states, whether they hold primaries or not. Similarly, a candidate's support across the entire nation can erode if his primary performance falls well below expectations. . . .

Without a series of state primaries, in which a relatively

[24] Michael Killan, "And Now a Word for Primaries," *Chicago Tribune*, April 2, 1972, pp. 5-6.

unknown candidate might dramatically demonstrate his growing popularity and appeal, it would be most difficult to come from far behind and win nomination. Established, well-known politicians would have an even stronger advantage over spokesmen for new groups and new ideas than they have had.[25]

There is certainly plenty of opportunity in the present system to build this kind of momentum: in 1976, for example, there were thirty primaries, held on thirteen different dates beginning on February 24 (New Hampshire) and ending on June 8 (California, New Jersey, and Ohio)—a period of fifteen weeks. There were also twenty-five first-level caucuses on sixteen dates, beginning on January 19 (Iowa) and ending on May 17 (Utah)—a period of seventeen weeks.

All the federalizing proposals would sharply reduce the number of dates available for building momentum. They therefore would make it very difficult—perhaps impossible—for an "outsider" like McGovern or Carter to win. They would also significantly increase the importance, already considerable, of what Arthur Hadley calls "the invisible primary"—the process by which certain aspirants emerge by the beginning of the presidential year as "the generally-recognized major contenders."[26] Political scientists have only begun to study this critical process, but it is clear that the news media play a major role, perhaps *the* major role, in separating the serious contenders from the many aspirants. Of course, the media also play a major role in determining as well as reporting the winners and losers in the long march through the present string of primaries. So it seems clear that any nominating system based mainly or wholly on primaries, whether decentralized or federalized, will be dominated by the media. We shall consider the consequences of this in a moment.

All primaries, whether decentralized or federalized, share at least one major defect as a method for choosing the best, or even the most-preferred candidate. A primary, like a referendum, is a device for registering and counting already-formed first preferences. It has no way of identifying, let alone aggregating, second and third choices so as to discover the candidate with the broadest—as opposed to the most intense—support. And since broad support is much better than narrow but intense support for unifying the party and appealing to

---

[25] William R. Keech and Donald R. Matthews, *The Party's Choice* (Washington, D.C.: The Brookings Institution, 1976), pp. 111, 245.

[26] Arthur T. Hadley, *The Invisible Primary* (Englewood Cliffs, N.J.: Prentice-Hall, Inc., 1976). See also Donald R. Matthews, "Presidential Nominations: Process and Outcomes," in James David Barber, ed., *Choosing the President* (Englewood Cliffs, N.J.: Prentice-Hall, Inc., 1974), pp. 36-70, esp. pp. 39-52.

the general electorate, this is a serious deficiency. As Wilson Carey McWilliams says, this trait is a

> *defect of the direct primary itself* when dealing with situa-
> tions where more than two candidates are in contention. The
> direct primary, like the Initiative and Referendum, is suc-
> cessful where questions can be formulated in "Yes" or "No"
> terms. It does not work where there are third alternatives
> and second choices. There, I need to do more than register
> a vote. I need to discuss, deliberate, make clear my own
> preferences and formulate alternative strategies. If I prefer
> Jackson among the announced candidates, it may be vital
> that I like Humphrey better, that I would rather have Carter
> than Frank Church, and so on.[27]

Some sort of proportional representation—perhaps the "alterna-
tive vote" system used in Australia—might remedy this deficiency:
Members of the Australian House of Representatives are elected from
single-member districts, as in the United States. But there is one
variation designed to ensure that no member is elected without the
approval of an absolute majority of voters. If a district's ballot con-
tains, say, four candidates for the one seat, the voters do not put an
"X" beside the name of the one they most prefer. Rather, they indicate their first, second, third, and fourth preferences by putting the
appropriate number beside each name. In the counting process, the
ballots are first sorted according to first preferences. If no candidate
has a majority, the candidate with the fewest first preferences is
dropped and his ballots are redistributed according to the second
preference indicated on each. This dropping and redistributing is con-
tinued until one candidate receives an absolute majority and is
elected.[28] Theoretically, there is no reason why this system could not
be used in a national presidential primary, but the chances that
Congress will enact any such system are too remote to bother with
here.

What kinds of candidates, then, are advantaged by the various
nominating systems used and proposed? The pre-1968 system was
dominated by state and regional party leaders, and they tended to

---

[27] McWilliams, "Down with Primaries," p. 429, italics in the original. See also
Jewell, "A Caveat on the Expanding Use of Presidential Primaries," pp. 280-281;
and Paul T. David, Ralph M. Goldman, and Richard C. Bain, *The Politics of
National Party Conventions* (Washington, D.C.: The Brookings Institution, 1960),
pp. 489-490.

[28] A handy description of the Australian system and its consequences is given in
Leon D. Epstein, "The Australian Political System," in Howard R. Penniman, ed.,
Australia at the Polls (Washington, D.C.: American Enterprise Institute, 1977),
pp. 30-33.

favor candidates they knew and trusted rather than those they did not know (or knew only too well)—Stevenson rather than Kefauver, Humphrey rather than McCarthy (but also Eisenhower rather than Taft). The 1972 system was dominated by issue and candidate activists, who favored candidates strongly committed to ideologies and causes rather than the less issue-oriented "pols"—McGovern rather than Humphrey or Muskie, Wallace rather than anyone else.

The 1976 system picked over 70 percent of the delegates in state primaries, strung out over a period of more than three months. This minimized the impact of local caucuses dominated by issue/candidate activists and maximized the impact of primaries conducted by ordinary voters and dominated by the mass media's portrayal of candidate images and identification of winners and losers. The 1976 system also operated in an atmosphere of diffuse disgust with the "Washington establishment," and together the system and the atmosphere favored nonstop campaigners and "outsiders" over federal officeholders—ex-Governor Carter won over Senators Jackson and Church and Representative Udall; ex-Governor Reagan nearly defeated incumbent President Ford.

Which way would a direct one-day national primary tilt? It most likely would favor candidates already well known through exposure in the national news media (since no outsider could make news by winning some early caucus or primary, as McGovern did in 1972 and Carter did in 1976)—say, Ted Kennedy and Jerry Brown over Wendell Anderson and David Obey, or Ronald Reagan over James Thompson, or any incumbent President over any challenger.

No doubt most of us can find some candidates we like and some we dislike in all these lists. So it seems that no system is guaranteed to produce—or freeze out—the kinds of candidates who please or repel us.

Impact on the Parties

Ever since the early 1830s, our national presidential political parties have lain dormant except for their quadrennial emergence to select and campaign for presidential candidates. Hence the national nominating conventions have been just about their only manifestation as anything other than free-floating labels. Even the recent enlargement of the Democratic National Committee and the Democrats' 1974 midterm convention have not challenged the national convention's preeminence as the national presidential party's ruling body. It is therefore appropriate to ask what would become of the parties' national conventions under each of the federalizing schemes.

The Udall-Ashbrook and Packwood proposals would affect the conventions very little. Most but not all of their delegates would be chosen by primaries. Most delegates would be bound by law to cast their convention votes for the candidates to whom they were legally pledged. The allocation of the delegates' presidential preferences in each state would be roughly proportional to the popular votes the candidates had received in the state's preferential poll. There would be some chance that no candidate would have the nomination locked up before the convention and that negotiating, arguing, and compromising at the convention would produce the winner. There would also be the likelihood that one candidate would emerge from the primaries so far ahead that most of his rivals would drop out and the convention would on its first ballot merely register a decision already made before it convened. There would even be a possibility—though certainly not a probability—that the number of states holding primaries would be reduced.

The Ottinger proposal would also preserve the convention's form, but all its delegates would be chosen by primaries and legally bound to certain candidates. The theoretical possibility would still exist that no aspirant would clinch the nomination before the convention and that the convention itself might choose the candidate by bargaining. But even more than under the Udall-Ashbrook or Packwood plans, the convention would be primarily a device for ratifying and legitimizing decisions already taken rather than a decision-making body.

The Quie proposal would strip the national conventions of their most important function—nominating presidential and vice-presidential candidates. The conventions could continue to perform their other traditional functions—writing platforms, adopting rules, launching campaigns. But the platforms would become even more indistinguishable from the presidential candidates' position papers; the rules would be subject to the candidate's de facto absolute veto; and the news media would not be inclined to give a campaign rally the gavel-to-gavel coverage they now give national conventions. It is highly doubtful whether either party would go to the considerable bother and expense of holding conventions with so little to do that would be significant or newsworthy.

If the foregoing analysis has any merit, then it seems that the Udall-Ashbrook and Packwood proposals would leave the national parties no weaker than they are now and would even leave open the possibility that they might get stronger. The state parties might be marginally weakened by the reduction or elimination of their power to set their states' primary dates as their own organizational and strategic needs might indicate. But the possibility of repealing state primary laws would remain, and hence also the possibility of the state parties' reasserting their influence over the choice of national convention delegations and the national nominee. The Ottinger proposal would weaken the national parties somewhat more and the state parties a good deal more by imposing primary selection of delegates on all of them with few if any prospects for rollbacks.

However, by far the most drastic impact on the parties, national and state, would come from the adoption of a national direct presidential primary. Let us remember that from its inception in the early 1900s to the present, the direct primary was not intended to be and has not been a device to make parties stronger and more responsible. It has rested upon the conviction that parties are at best interlopers between the sovereign people and their elected officials and at worst rapacious enemies of honest and responsive government. In a word, primaries were adopted not to make good parties even better, but to make them less evil by wrenching away their most important power. One of the greatest early advocates of primaries, Senator George W. Norris (Republican, Nebraska), minced no words on the point. He was quite sure, he said, that the direct primary weakens party control and responsibility. Fine!

> I frankly offer [this result] as one of the best reasons for its retention. The direct primary will lower party responsibility. In its stead it establishes individual responsibility. It does lessen allegiance to party and increases individual independence, both as to the public official and as to the private citizen. It takes away the power of the party leader or boss and places the responsibility for control upon the individual. It lessens party spirit and decreases partisanship. These are some of the reasons why the primary should be retained and extended.[29]

In the opinion of most observers (including this one), the direct primary has weakened the parties in most states much as Norris hoped it would. As V.O. Key summed it up:

> The adoption of the direct primary opened the road for disruptive forces that gradually fractionalized the party organization. By permitting more effective direct appeals by individual politicians to the party membership, the primary system freed forces driving toward the disintegration of party organizations and facilitated the construction of factions and cliques attached to the ambitions of individual

---

[29] George W. Norris, "Why I Believe in the Direct Primary," *Annals of the American Academy of Political and Social Science*, vol. 106 (March 1923), p. 23.

leaders. The convention system compelled leaders to treat, to deal, to allocate nominations; the primary permits individual aspirants by one means or another to build a wider following within the party. . . .

Indeed, the fact that aspirants for nomination must cultivate the rank and file makes it difficult to maintain an organizational core dedicated to the party as such; instead, leadership energies operate to construct activist clusters devoted to the interests of particular individuals.[30]

The primary's disruptive effects that Key describes have already seriously weakened our national parties and their state affiliates. If we force the national parties to perform their most important function in the hostile environment of a national direct primary, we may well reduce them to being no more than labels automatically awarded to the two winners of the national votes. What benefit of a national primary is worth that cost?

---

[30] V. O. Key, Jr., *Politics, Parties and Pressure Groups*, 5th ed. (New York: Thomas Y. Crowell, 1964), pp. 342, 386.

5
Costs and Benefits of Shifting the Federal Balance

Each of the four proposals we have considered increases to some degree the federal government's power to control the procedures for selecting the nominees for our most important elective office. There is certainly nothing novel or revolutionary in shifting the federal balance away from the states to Washington—or transferring the power to control party affairs away from party organizations to legislatures and courts. We have done both many times in our history because we believed the anticipated benefits of the shifts would more than justify the constitutional, social, economic, and political costs. Sometimes we were right and sometimes we were not. But we must always make the calculation as best we can. Thus it seems appropriate to conclude this paper by reviewing both the benefits claimed and the costs alleged for federalized presidential primaries—concentrating mainly, though not exclusively, on the proposals for a one-day direct national primary.

Benefits

(1) Uniformity and Simplicity. At present, each state decides for itself whether to hold a presidential primary and, if so, under what rules. One result is such a wide variety of rules that most summaries despair of general categories and describe the rules state by state. Another is the fact that election results mean different things in different states. In New York, for example, it is possible to estimate how many delegates expressing a preference for each aspirant have been elected and therefore who "won"; but the votes are counted in such a way that it is not possible to say how many individual votes each aspirant's delegate-candidates collectively won in the whole state. In New

Hampshire, on the other hand, it is clear how many votes each aspirant has won in the presidential preference poll (which gets by far the most attention from the news media), but it is difficult to learn how many pledged delegates—who are chosen in a separate election—each aspirant has won.

The state laws, then, provide nothing resembling a uniform or clear scoring system. Hence the news media's interpretation of the results becomes the de facto scoring system, which is one of the factors making the media critical actors in the presidential nominating process.

This state of affairs could, of course, be changed by state cooperation. If all the states holding primaries would agree on the dates and the rules, the nation could have uniformity without federalization. But this is so unlikely it is not worth discussing. In 1976, the idea was put to a small test when a number of states, especially in New England and the Far West, talked of holding regional primaries on common dates. But in the New England region, New Hampshire refused to surrender its choice position as the first state in the union to hold a primary. Vermont adopted a primary procedure quite different from those in the other states, and Connecticut failed to adopt any kind of primary. In the West, Idaho, Nevada, and Oregon got together on May 25, but Montana held out for June 1 and California for June 8, while the whole idea was rejected by Alaska, Arizona, Colorado, Hawaii, New Mexico, Utah, Washington, and Wyoming.

Federalization of the rules will change this, it is contended. The more federalized the rules are, the greater will be the uniformity among the states. And a direct national primary will, of course, mean that one and only one set of rules will govern the selection process across the nation. This will still not eliminate the news media's role entirely—after all, they will surely continue to report who is ahead and who is behind prior to the national primary. But at least they will become reporters more than scorekeepers.

Many advocates of federalized primaries feel that achieving a uniform, unambiguous set of rules is in itself sufficient justification for their proposals. The present system's unconscionable complexity, they say, has several pernicious effects which only uniform federal rules can eliminate. For one, the endless interstate variations in the present rules require all serious candidates to maintain stables of experts to lead them through the mazes the rules create. If there were only one set of rules—say, a simple one-day national primary—the candidates could reduce or even eliminate at least this part of their organizations. This argument seems persuasive, although it is not clear how great a contribution eliminating these rules experts would make to the national welfare (or, for that matter, to white-collar unemployment).

A stronger claim is made for the benefits accruing to ordinary voters: the complexity of the present mélange of rules baffles the voters; they do not bother to participate in a system they cannot understand; hence popular alienation rises and voting turnouts decline. If we simplify the rules and make them the same everywhere, voters will understand them and will feel more like participating.

There may be something to this, marginally at least. My study of participation in the 1976 presidential nominations showed that voter turnout in the primaries was, by a small margin, highest in the states in which the presidential preference poll results were binding on all the delegates of both parties and lowest in the states in which the preference poll results were advisory only. But the average turnout was 44.9 percent in the former states to 41.0 percent in the latter, not a huge difference.[31] All the other factors that combine to keep turnouts in primary elections much lower than those in general elections should continue to operate. So it seems likely that complete federalization of presidential primaries would increase voting turnout by a few percentage points—an improvement, no doubt, but hardly a great leap forward.

(2) Equal Weighting of Votes. Under the present presidential nominating system, each state decides for itself when its primary will be held. Inevitably, different states choose different dates, and in 1976, as we have seen, the result was thirty primaries held on thirteen different dates beginning in New Hampshire on February 24 and ending in California, New Jersey, and Ohio on June 8. One important result of this decentralized date selection is the fact that the votes cast in the earlier primaries have a considerably greater impact on the outcome than votes cast in the later primaries. The reason is simple: the candidate who does well (or, more accurately, the candidate who the news media says has done well) in the early primaries becomes the "front runner." And this brings him financial support, media attention, name recognition, and an aura of success that make for success in later primaries. When this "momentum" is combined with the proportionality or "fair reflection" rules, which guarantee the early front runner sizable blocs of delegates from later primaries even in states

---

[31] Ranney, *Participation*, pp. 27-28.

where he finishes only second or third in the preferential polls,[32] it makes the fast start almost irresistible. Hence the early primaries are far more critical than the late ones.

New Hampshire and California are prime examples. For decades, New Hampshire has jealously guarded its position as the first state to hold a primary each presidential year. In 1976, its voters cast a microscopic 0.6 percent of all the votes cast in the Democratic primaries and chose 0.6 percent of the Democratic delegates and 0.9 percent of the Republican delegates. Yet Carter's victory (he led a field of five with 29 percent of the votes) made him the front runner in the media's eyes, and Ford's edge over Reagan (50.6 percent in a two-man race) was said to put him well in the lead. Nor was this the first time New Hampshire had been so important. In 1968, Eugene McCarthy launched his strong though ultimately unsuccessful drive for the Democratic nomination with an unexpectedly strong showing in the New Hampshire primary, and in 1972, George McGovern started from a similar base to go all the way to the nomination.

By contrast, consider California. In 1976, Californians cast 20 percent of all votes cast in the nation's primaries and elected 9 percent of the Democratic delegates and 7 percent of the Republican delegates. Yet neither selected a winner: the Democrats gave Edmund ("Jerry") Brown 59 percent to Carter's 20 percent, while the Republicans gave Reagan 66 percent to Ford's 34 percent. But it really didn't matter: Carter had the nomination locked up long before the California primary, and Ford was thought to be well ahead after New Hampshire. In the end, both won.

Take it a bit further. In 1976, Carter was generally—and, as it turned out, correctly—believed to have the nomination clinched after he defeated Jackson in the Pennsylvania primary of April 27. At that point, only seven states had voted, with an aggregate total of 8,181,169 votes—28 percent of the 28,925,253 votes eventually cast in all thirty primaries. But clearly the early 28 percent had considerably more impact than the later 72 percent on who won the Democratic nomination. The Republican situation was less clear because of the extreme

---

[32] Rule 11 of the Democratic party's rules for selecting delegates to the 1976 national convention stipulated that: "At all stages of the delegate selection process, delegations shall be allocated in a fashion that fairly reflects the expressed presidential preference, uncommitted, or no preference status of the primary voters, or . . . the convention and caucus participants, except that preferences securing less than 15 percent (15%) of the votes cast for the delegation need not be awarded any delegates": *Delegate Selection Rules for the 1976 Democratic National Convention* (Washington, D.C.: Democratic National Committee, 1975), p. 6.

closeness of the race, but even there Ford's early victories seem to have helped him more than Reagan's late victories helped him.

There can be little doubt, then, that in the present system votes in the earlier primaries weigh more heavily in the national outcome than those in the later ones. The proposals for regional primaries with randomly selected dates would not eliminate the greater weighting of votes in the earlier primaries; they would merely randomize the advantage and pass it around among the regions. The one-day national primary would, of course, eliminate entirely any timing advantage for any state or region. That might or might not result in better campaigns or superior nominees. But by the familiar criterion of one man/one vote, it is hard to justify the special weight the earlier primaries enjoy under the present system or would continue to enjoy under the proposals for regional primaries.

(3) Better Campaigns. Most advocates of federalized primaries stress the need to reduce the inordinate physical strain and financial burdens of campaigning in the present system. The wide geographical and temporal scattering of the states' primaries, they say, requires the candidates to keep crisscrossing the continent. This makes for high travel costs and severe physical strain on the candidates—so much so that, in Polsby and Wildavsky's well-known aside, "the United States might have to restrict its presidential candidates to wealthy athletes."[33]

This argument is less than overwhelming. The federal regulation and financing of presidential primary campaigns, inaugurated in 1976 and now well established, will control costs in future campaigns under any kind of primary system. And while one's heart goes out to the overworked candidates, one is hard pressed to name any aspirants who balked at entering or later withdrew from the race because it was too tiring. Perhaps, indeed, anyone seeking the most demanding elective office in the world *should* prove that he or she can stand more physical and psychological stress than most of us.

(4) Better Representation. In the end, the most powerful claim made for federalized primaries is that they will provide better representation—better in two senses of the term: the electorate in a federalized system will more closely resemble the rank-and-file identifiers of each party than any national convention ever has or ever will; and a national primary is more likely than a convention to choose the nominee most preferred by the rank and file.

---

[33] Polsby and Wildavsky, *Presidential Elections*, p. 222. See also Senator Packwood's remarks in the *Congressional Record*, April 1, 1977, p. S5324.

As to the first claim, Democratic or Republican convention delegates, whether handpicked by party bosses or chosen by middle-class activists in participatory caucuses, are richer, better educated, more knowledgeable, and ideologically more intense and more extreme than the ordinary identifiers in their respective parties. As we have seen, the same discrepancies exist between each party's primary voters and its nonvoting identifiers, but the differences are generally smaller than those between identifiers and convention delegates. Accordingly, the larger the number of people actively selecting each party's presidential nominee, the more closely they are likely to resemble the party's rank and file in the sense of sharing the same socioeconomic characteristics and views on the questions of the day. And, if this is correct, the system likely to produce the most representative "selectorate" of all is the one-day national direct primary.

This logic seems to me faultless and the conclusion correct, *provided* we understand that even in a one-day direct national primary the electorate is likely to consist of less than half of the nation's citizens of voting age. Experience in the states suggests that the primary turnout will be no more than half as large as that in the ensuing general election. Hence, so long as turnouts in general elections continue to range between 53 percent and 61 percent, as they have since 1952, we can expect turnouts in direct national primaries to range between 25 percent and 30 percent. This is a lot more people than have participated up to now—but still a number small enough to make it unlikely that they will be greatly more representative than the present "selectorate."

But, proponents of federalization avow, a national primary would be more representative in a much more important sense: it would be more likely to choose the candidates preferred by most rank-and-file party identifiers. To assess this claim, we must first ask: How well have the conventions performed in this regard? If we measure the preferences of the rank and file by using the results of the public opinion polls' soundings of party identifiers, the conventions have done very well. As Keech and Matthews sum up the record:

> The presidential nominees over the past forty years have been with remarkable regularity the leaders of the final pre-convention poll of their party's rank and file. The only clear exception to this pattern is Stevenson in 1952, who trailed far behind Kefauver. Three other cases are close or ambiguous. In 1940 Dewey led the last poll before the convention, but he was clearly slipping fast; Willkie led in the final poll, taken during the convention. In 1964, Goldwater was tied for first at 22 percent in the final poll; all told, four

candidates had between 20 percent and 22 percent support from the GOP rank and file. McGovern's lead in the final 1972 poll was narrow. If second and third choices had been taken into account, some other candidate might well have stood higher on the average in these last two cases (and perhaps a few others as well). Nevertheless, even though the party rank and file does not directly make the nominating decision, the results have been remarkably congruent with their preferences.[34]

Thus only in 1952 would a national primary probably have chosen a candidate different from the one selected by the convention: it would have picked the people's choice (Kefauver) rather than the bosses' choice (Stevenson). In other words, twenty-two conventions have been held since the public opinion polls first gave us a good measure of rank-and-file presidential preferences (1936 to 1976), and twenty-one of those conventions have nominated the first choices of the parties' identifiers.[35] In most leagues, a batting average of .955 is considered quite good, and certainly not an urgent reason to change the lineup.

In sum: the federalization of presidential primaries would probably yield some benefits, though not in such numbers or richness as its proponents claim. The unwarranted special influence of states holding early primaries would be weakened, passed around, or eliminated. The rules would be marginally more simple and the game easier to follow, with perhaps some modest resulting gains in popular participation and confidence in the process. The candidates would probably travel somewhat less and rest somewhat more. Control of nominations would probably be removed from party bosses and ideological activists.

Not bad. But in presidential politics, as in all other facets of life, every benefit has its costs. How many and how burdensome are likely to be the costs of federalized primaries?

Costs

(1) Further Dismantling of the Parties. Most analysts agree that since 1968 American political parties have been greatly weakened, especially

---

[34] Keech and Matthews, *The Party's Choice*, p. 215.

[35] Keech and Matthews's analysis covers the period from 1936 to 1972. In 1976, the last Gallup preconvention polls showed Carter in the lead with 53 percent (he was nominated with 74 percent of the Democratic Convention's first-ballot votes) and Ford ahead with 57 percent to Reagan's 37 percent (Ford was nominated by the Republicans with 52.5 percent of the first ballot votes to Reagan's 47.4 percent).

at the presidential level. It is not always clear, however, just what is meant by "weakened," so let me explain how I use the term.

A strong presidential party, in my view, would be led by a mix of national and state party leaders—governors, state chairs, state legislative leaders, U.S. senators and representatives, national chairs, Presidents and ex-Presidents—whose influence with the national convention's delegates was so strong that when a coalition of leaders agreed on who the candidate should be, the delegates would follow their lead and choose him. The coalition would also see to it that the party's platform would help to unite the party and put it in the best possible position to win the election. Some of the leaders making up a particular coalition would drop out and others join from one convention to the next, but coalitions and their powers and functions would persist.

Such coalitions, I believe, nominated Hubert Humphrey and Richard Nixon in 1968, Richard Nixon in 1960, Dwight Eisenhower and Adlai Stevenson in 1952, Thomas Dewey in 1944 and 1948, and all candidates other than incumbent Presidents (who were all but automatically renominated) before 1944. John Kennedy in 1960 used his victories in the primaries to convince skeptical party leaders that a Catholic could be elected President. But the only clear case of an outsider's overpowering a party establishment prior to 1972 came in 1964 when Barry Goldwater's conservative enthusiasts captured the nomination despite the opposition of most established Republican leaders.

The 1972 Democratic convention was the first held under the McGovern-Fraser commission's new rules. Those rules, as we have seen, were intended to strip the nominating power from the traditional coalitions of party leaders and hand it over to persons enthusiastic and active in their support for a candidate or a cause, though not necessarily experienced in or committed to the party. In 1972 there were many such activists, and most were dedicated to either George McGovern or George Wallace. McGovern's were much better organized, and they won him the nomination. In 1976, the Mikulski commission's "fair reflection" rule and the proliferation of state primaries put the nominating power beyond the reach of both the party regulars and the issue/candidate enthusiasts, and it passed to the entrepreneurial candidate organizations, especially the well-organized Jimmy Carter enterprise. Carter began his campaign almost unknown to the Democrats' established leaders, but, far from being a handicap, his status as a party outsider was a substantial part of his appeal to primary voters—and in 1976 the primaries were where most of the

34

action was. The result is that under the present rules, no strong presidential party, as I have defined it, is likely to rise again.

Thus, since 1968 the national parties have been greatly weakened by a series of wounds, some self-inflicted and some inflicted by outside blows. Jeane Kirkpatrick's recent survey of these traumas identifies as the main external causes the rise of the counterculture, the declining prestige of material incentives, the declining popular confidence in all political institutions, the proliferation of presidential primaries, and the public financing of presidential nominating and electing campaigns. She also lists a number of the parties' self-inflicted wounds: the McGovern-Fraser rules transferring power from party regulars to ideological activists, the prohibition of guaranteed delegate posts for party leaders, the express or implied quotas for women, blacks, and youth among convention delegates, and the requirement of proportional representation of preferences for presidential candidates in the national conventions.[36]

In some respects, the recent proliferation of presidential primaries is one of the effects of these underlying causes. Yet it has also been a cause of the parties' debilitation. We should be clear that direct primaries are, in intention and effect, devices for bypassing political parties in the performance of their most crucial function, the making of nominations. It follows that the greater the role played by primaries in presidential nominations, the weaker will be the role played by the parties. If that is correct, then the Udall-Ashbrook and Packwood proposals would probably leave the national parties little weaker than now (which, admittedly, is not saying very much). By at least permitting states which now have primaries to repeal them, these plans even leave open the possibility, however faint, that the primaries might diminish and the parties get stronger.

The Ottinger proposal, on the other hand, would require that *all* delegates be chosen by primaries; the Quie proposal would remove all intermediaries between the voters and the nomination and would probably lead to the complete abolition of national conventions. Either proposal, in my judgment, would make the national parties nothing more than labels automatically awarded to the primary winners.

The parties are very sick now. Some analysts believe their sickness is mortal, and they may be right. But if either the Ottinger or the Quie plan is adopted, they will surely die. If we stay our hands from delivering the final blow, we at least leave open the possibility that some day they may recover. Believing, as I do, that political parties

---

[36] Jeane Jordan Kirkpatrick, *Dismantling the Parties: Reflections on Party Reform and Party Decomposition* (Washington, D.C.: American Enterprise Institute, 1978).

have been invaluable aggregating, moderating, consensus-building agencies in all democratic polities, especially our own, I can only conclude that dismantling them even further by a universal federalized primary would be a cost far greater than any benefit or set of benefits such a primary could possibly bring.

(2) Aggrandizing the Media. There are about 90 million Americans who fulfill the constitutional qualifications for the presidency. Since this is clearly an impossibly large number of alternatives to choose among, there must be some nominating system, some agency or agencies to reduce the theoretical 90 million possibilities to a manageable "short list" of fifteen or twenty from whom the major parties' candidates are actually chosen. Presidential nominating politics, like other parts of nature, abhors a vacuum. If a national direct primary would, as I have argued, effectively remove the party organizations from any active role in the sifting and winnowing process, we need to ask what would take their place.

Persons who thought of themselves as serious presidential possibilities would, of course, start the process themselves by deciding to enter the race or stay out. For those who took the plunge, the candidates' organizations would continue to act as entrepreneurs seeking endorsements, contributions, publicity, and votes for their champions as in the past. But they would contribute mainly to the process of what goes into the hopper, not what comes out.

National interest groups, such as the Women's Political Caucus, the Right to Life Committee, the Black Caucus, and the AFL-CIO, would continue their traditional efforts to trade endorsements and contributions for policy stands and personnel promises. But such groups have never demonstrated much ability to influence the outcome of primary elections, so their impact on the sifting and winnowing would be minor at best.

In my judgment, the clear gainers in influence from the dismantling of the party organizations would be the national news media—the national television and radio networks, the major newspapers, and the wire services. As we have seen, their interpretations of the state primaries and caucuses, especially the early ones, already have a powerful influence on who wins and who loses.[37] Powerful though they now are, however, the media are still limited by the facts: they can hardly comment that Jackson's showing in the New Hamp-

---

[37] For a stimulating discussion of this influence, see Michael J. Robinson, "Television and American Politics, 1956–1976," *The Public Interest* (Summer, 1977), pp. 3-39.

shire primary was poor if he was not even entered, nor can they report that Bayh is gaining momentum if he has already announced his withdrawal. In a national direct primary, on the other hand, the only preelection facts relevant to who was winning would be public opinion polls and estimates of the sizes of crowds at candidates' meetings. The former are scientifically more respectable than the latter, but neither constitutes hard data in the sense that election returns do. And hard data of that sort would be available only after national primary day. Thus, a one-day national direct primary would give the news media even more power than they now have to influence the outcomes of contests for nominations by shaping most people's perceptions of how these contests were proceeding.

It seems to me that the news media, especially the television networks, are not ideally suited for this kind of power—not because they lie, cheat, or seek control of nominations, but because their competitive situations impel them to portray nominating contests in a way that works against the kind of bargaining, consensus, and moderation which characterized the process dominated by the party organizations. The prime object of all networks, private or public, is to attract the largest possible number of viewers. The way to do that, they say, is to report the news—to tell what is really going on. But what is the networks' idea of news? Almost always it is some form of conflict, and the networks can be counted on to seek it out in interviews on the convention floor if it cannot be found (as it usually cannot) on the podium.

All this, no doubt, helps to improve the appeal and salability of presidential nominating politics as a spectator sport. But it is hardly conducive to the negotiations, bargaining, and compromises on which strong political parties rely for choosing their nominees and uniting behind them. With the national parties destroyed as anything more than labels, presidential nominations consisting of competition among entrepreneurial candidate organizations as interpreted and shaped by the national news media might well be very much like the one-party —and therefore no-party—politics of the old South described so memorably by V.O. Key:

> When one-party factionalism is reduced to a few adjectives descriptive of its form—multifaceted, discontinuous, kaleido-scopic, fluid, transient—it becomes in appearance a matter of no particular import. Nevertheless, these characteristics point to weaknesses of profound significance in one-party factions as instruments of popular leadership and, by contrast, point to the extraordinary importance in the workings of popular government of political parties, imperfect though they may

be. Although it is the custom to belittle the contributions of American parties, their performance seems heroic alongside that of a pulverized factionalism.

In an atomized and individualistic politics it becomes a matter of each leader for himself and often for himself only for the current campaign. Individualistic or disorganized politics places a high premium on demogogic qualities of personality that attract voter-attention. Party machinery, in the advancement of leaders, is apt to reject those with rough edges and angular qualities out of preference for more conformist personalities. Perhaps the necessities of an unorganized politics—lacking in continuing divisions of the electorate and in continuing collaboration of party workers —provide a partial explanation for the rise of power of some of the spectacular southern leaders.[38]

Presidential politics, 1984?

(3) Ending Experiments. Earlier we discussed uniformity of rules as one of the benefits claimed for federalized presidential primaries. Benefit it may be, but there are costs as well—costs that rise in proportion to the degree of federalization. One such cost is the loss of the states' present role as "laboratories" for testing various kinds of primary and caucus systems. The present variations in the states' rules enable us to observe the impact of particular rules—for example, closed versus crossover voting, binding versus advisory preference polls, proportional representation versus winner-take-all—on such matters as voting turnout and types of candidates favored.[39] If the rules become exactly the same over the entire nation, we shall no longer be able to analyze the consequences of these variations. Thus our ability to identify causal connections between particular rules and political outcomes we do not like will largely disappear. And if we have one and only one set of rules for the entire nation, it had better be the right set.

---

[38] V. O. Key, Jr., *Southern Politics in State and Nation* (New York: Alfred A. Knopf, 1949), pp. 302-303, 304-305.

[39] For examples of such analyses, see Ranney, *Participation*; James I. Lengle and Byron Shafer, "Primary Rules, Political Power, and Social Change," *American Political Science Review*, vol. 70 (March 1976), pp. 25-40; and Gerald W. Pomper, "New Rules and New Games in the National Conventions," paper presented at the Annual Meeting of the American Political Science Association, Washington, D.C., 1977.

6
Conclusion

In my judgment, the probable costs of federalizing our presidential primaries are greater and more certain than the benefits claimed for doing so. And the greater the degree of federalization the greater will be the excess of costs over benefits. The Udall-Ashbrook proposal would affect the national and state parties relatively little, though it would severely limit each state party's ability to choose a primary date most desirable for its special purposes. The proposal might even help the national parties marginally by encouraging a few states to drop their primaries (would New Hampshire keep its primary if it could no longer be the first in the field?) and by reducing an outsider's ability to build up momentum by a series of wins in scattered early primaries. The Packwood-Hatfield-Stevens plan would strip the state parties of any power to time the primaries to suit their best interests, but otherwise should have about the same consequences as Udall-Ashbrook.

The Ottinger and Quie plans, however, would impose uniform primary rules on all states and end any participation in presidential nominations through caucus systems. The Quie proposal would even ignore state lines in the casting of the votes and thus in campaigning, building support, and forming coalitions. The consequence, I believe, would be a great weakening of the state parties and a virtual end to the national parties as anything more than passive arenas for contests between entrepreneurial candidate organizations.

Probably no formal constitutional amendment would be required to bring about any of these changes. But if made, they would surely constitute as great an alteration in our party system and in our way of choosing our President as the change made in the early 1800s— also without formal amendments—when the rise of political parties converted the electoral college into an instrument for popular election of the President. Most Americans would surely agree that we should not lightly make the change to federalized primaries. I believe we should not make it at all.